LAURENCE LEONARD DOWLING

A man for all seasons.

Dr Patricia Sherwood

Text: copyright: Patricia Sherwood

All rights reserved. No part may be copied without prior permission of the author or acknowledgement of source.

ISBN: **978-0-9876143-7-7**
Sophia Publications, Bunbury, 2022

Layout: Manish Pathak
Cover image: pexels.com

DEDICATION

To my father and all my paternal ancestors who have endured so much for so many generations, that I might be privileged to live the life of freedom and abundance that I enjoy today.

And for all the genes and traits, they have gifted me particularly determination to overcome the insurmountable, courage to face the challenges of life, a spirit to survive adversities, quick thinking and acting in a crisis, the ability to seize the moment, to speak up for the poor and oppressed, a kindness of heart, a sensitivity of soul which makes poets, dreamers, as well as leaders and indomitable survivors.

And most especially to David John Laurence, my son who inspired me to write this biography of the grandfather whom he has never known, but from whom he has inherited some of his finest traits and qualities. Without his insistence and encouragement this book would never have been born.

PREFACE

Laurence Leonard Dowling was a man of few words but with a history of life experience that is testimony to the troubled times in which he lived: the Great Depression, the Second World War and the unaddressed problems of a wartime survivor. A childhood of poverty, schooled in a life of hard knocks, he remained a stoical survivor despite life's many adversities. As my father, he inspired my love for the Australian bush, gifted me with his love of Australian poets, the stars, flowers and the natural world. This biography is based upon fragments of his life that he shared, my mother recalled or his younger sister Joan contributed but essentially it remains my perception of him, as my father, a soldier, a man of action, an incisive thinker, a jack of all trades, a survivor of poverty and adversity, a sensitive soul, a poet and a dreamer even in his darkest hours. He remains an inspiration to my soul and will always remain in my heart as a "man for all seasons."

CONTENTS

Dedication iii
Preface v

Chapter 1: The Dowlings: mavericks, miners and migrants 1
Chapter 2: Laurie's Childhood and Youth: Albany and Northam. ... 13
Chapter 3: The War and its Fallout 29
Chapter 4: A Second Start: marriage and a new family. 37

CHAPTER 1

THE DOWLINGS: MAVERICKS, MINERS AND MIGRANTS

The Dowlings hail from the Emerald Isle, true blood Irish for generations. The surname was first found in Westmeath in the Irish Midlands, province of Leinster where they held a family seat in ancient times. They claim descent from the Heremon Kings of Ireland and were chiefs in County Wicklow for generations. Today they are found in the southern counties of Ireland especially Cork, Laois, Leinster and Kilkenny.

The Dowling crest reflects this grand heritage with a shield representing a chief with wisdom and a lion representing courage, an oak tree representing antiquity and strength and colours representing loyalty and generosity. The Gaelic form of the name is O Dubhlaoich which means dark featured, great, prodigious and a hero or champion contrasted with the assigned English meaning of the name as "stupid".

Laurence Leonard Dowling: *A man for all seasons.*

The Anglo Saxon invasion of Ireland begun in the 12 th century, was accelerated in the early 17th century when they sought to reduce it to a colony. In 1609 leading members of the Dowling clan were transplanted to Tarbert on the border of north Kerry and west Limerick for riotous and politically disturbing behaviours. The next centuries were to see the Irish people reduced to poverty, starvation and political suppression by English Lords who seized the lands and assets of the country and enslaved the population to work for a pittance. Little remained of the grand Dowling ancestry but the qualities of courage, generosity, leadership and strength.

Laurence Dowling's recent ancestors eked a living through work in hard rock mining on the Allihies copper mine on the west coast of Cork. The mine was started by an English industrialist, Puxley in 1812 and continued until 1884. Situated on the scenic Beara peninsula on the west coast of Cork, this mine heralded the industrial revolution for this area. Despite the beauty of the peninsula facing the wild Atlantic Ocean, the working conditions for the underground miners were dismal and the wages low.

Image 1: Allihies copper mine, Beara, Cork.
Ref: http://bearabaoitours.com/copper-mine-tour/

Dr Patricia Sherwood

It was dangerous and difficult work and if a man survived to 30 or 40 years of age he did well. Women and children worked above the ground crushing rocks that had been mined. The crushed ore was shipped to Swansea for processing. The miners and their families who survived were physically tough and hardy but it was a subsistence rather than a living existence. Housing was short and it is estimated that there were over twenty five inhabitants for each house. (https://acmm.ie/theminemuseum/). The underground mines were prone to flooding and the working conditions were harsh and dangerous with little respite for miners or families.

Within a few decades the Dowling ancestors of Laurence Dowling, left Cork and the Beara mine and migrated to the work in the copper mines of Cornwell, also hard rock mining, where they hoped for better lives for their families. The owners and bosses of the mines were English, but the labourers were predominately Irish migrants.

Image 2: the Cornwall mines
Ref: https://www.cornwallforever.co.uk/history/1815-1920-the-great-emigration

Laurence Leonard Dowling: *A man for all seasons.*

These migrants were tough but they were also dreamers and poets and visionaries and never lost hope in a better future. As Catholic, poor, and sub class citizens, skilled only in mining, they dreamed of finding gold, the one thing their mining talents could achieve that could lead them out of poverty . John James Dowling's father, Edward James made the decision in the 1840s to join the exodus of miners to Australia.

Image 3: Bendigo Australia
Ref: http://www.worldeasyguides.com/australia/bendigo/where-is-bendigo-on-map-australia/

It was a courageous move given that the English/ Irish divide had been transplanted from England to Australia and employment opportunities were limited:

Dr Patricia Sherwood

From the First Fleet to the 1960s, Irish Catholics were a discriminated-against underclass, openly barred from employment in much of the private sector and accused of disloyalty for putting Australia before the British Empire. In what we now cozily term "Anglo-Celtic" Australia, a virtual social apartheid existed at times between Catholics and Protestants. But the divisions were not about religion. They derived from England's colonial oppression of Ireland, grievances transplanted to Australia and nurtured with bitterness by both sides."This is a Protestant country and it is our pride that we have absolute liberty under the Union Jack," declared E.K Bowden, minister for defence, in 1922. Four years earlier, in late 1918, an Irish Catholic priest in Sydney, one Dr Patrick Tuomey, was fined £30 for sedition for criticising the British presence in Ireland; he thereby "by word of mouth encouraged disloyalty to the British Empire". (Siobhan McHugh, 2009, **The Sydney Morning Herald.** *How the Irish rose above Australia's social apartheid.*)

Edward James was not deterred and in the tradition of the poor Irish decided to take his chances as a miner. Stopping briefly in South Australia, he settled in Victoria, in the heart of the first great Australian gold rush: Eaglehawk Nest near Bendigo. My father's grandfather, John James was born in 1848. He married Emily Doyle and they had four children also in Eaglehawk. His son, John James junior, born in 1887 was Laurie's father and my grandfather. They all had gold in their veins, and it rushed through their blood and filtered into my father's DNA. Bendigo breathed the life of gold rushes, gold affluence, riches sought and riches banished and above all it bred the euphoria of golden dreams.

Image 4: Bendigo gold mines in the 1850s
Ref: https://earthresources.vic.gov.au/geologyexploration/minerals/metals/gold/gold-mining-in-victoria/gold-mines

Bendigo was known as tent city and between 1851 and 1900 it yielded the majority of the world's supply of gold. People from all over the world flooded into Bendigo and it was not until the 1900s that reserves began to be exhausted. As the gold mines in Bendigo were running down, the young John James Dowling with gold fever in his blood, headed west to Kalgoorlie and Coolgardie to join the gold rushes in Western Australia. He was around the age of 20 years.

Image 5: map showing Kalgoorlie and Norseman in relation to Perth
Ref: https://www.gallivantingoz.com.au/
suggested-travel-routes/perth-sw-circuit/

On the train at Southern Cross, a remote station on the way to Coolgardie and 200 miles west of Kalgoorlie, he met Ellen Burns Pedlar. She was of Scottish descent, a Glaswegian and her grandmother had been a waiting lady for Lady Macarthur, the wife of the famous pastoralist John Macarthur of New South Wales.

Laurence Leonard Dowling: *A man for all seasons.*

Image 6: Grandmother of Ellen Burns: lady in waiting for John Macarthur's wife. 1820's, NSW.

Ellen's mother had married a miner from Broken Hill where Ellen was born. Her family had joined the gold rushes to Kalgoorlie in the 1900's, like so many families from around the world. Ellen was a stunningly beautiful 15 year old young woman and she won the heart of the young John James Dowling.

Image 7: Ellen Burns Pedlar's mother, Laurie's maternal grandmother.

At the age of 21 years, John James married Ellen Burns Pedlar at Saint Matthew's Church of England Boulder in 1908, an excellent compromise for a Methodist and a Roman Catholic. They were in love and courageous, defying social norms that argued that a Protestant and Catholic marriage was unacceptable and unsustainable. They agreed that the boys would be Catholic and the girls Methodist and they had a long lasting relationship producing 14 children, of whom

3 died at birth or shortly afterwards. The first four were born in Kalgoorlie in the heyday of the gold rush.

Image 8: Kalgoorlie main street 1900s
Ref: https://historicalcycleclub.com.au/hidden/goldfields

John James worked as a miner and although the town was prospering to the extent that it even had its own opera theatre and wealthy hotels built with grandeur and style, a miner's wages were a pittance and food and water was extremely costly. The surrounding affluence was a constant reminder of the poverty of the unsuccessful miners and labourers. The hotels in particular reeked of the new found moneyed elite. President Hoover worked as a mining engineer in the town before he was president, and donated a magnificent fire place architrave with mirror to his lover, a barmaid which still has pride of place in one of Kalgoorlie's, grandest old hotels "the Palace."

It was built in 1897 and designed to be the most luxurious hotel outside of Perth. Grand hotels decorated Hannan Street and the gold euphoria gave an ambience to the town, as if the streets were paved with gold.

Image 9: the grand Exchange hotel in Kalgoorlie, 1900s
Ref: https://en.wikipedia.org/wiki/File:Exchange_Hotel_Kalgoorlie.jpg

Home for the first four children in the Dowling family was Kalgoorlie but then it became obvious that gold mining would not support the rapidly growing family, John James abandoned a long tradition of miners, and decided to apply for a job as a locomotive driver. He was stationed in Albany, a beautiful coastal town on the south coast of Western Australia. The climate was temperate and a relief after the harsh climatic conditions in Kalgoorlie.

Laurence Leonard Dowling: *A man for all seasons.*

Image 10: Albany in the 1900s: a port city.
Ref: https://friendsofalbanyhistory.wordpress.com/tag/early-1900s/

Water was abundant and food much cheaper than in Kalgoorlie, as this temperate climate was abundant with rainfall and supported a wide variety of agriculture and horticulture. Albany looked like the ideal place to raise their rapidly expanding family. Located facing the southern ocean, Albany boasted abundant fishing and whaling industries which were part of the town's livelihood. The Dowlings arrived with high hopes for a better lifestyle and more abundant nourishment than Kalgoorlie offered.

CHAPTER 2

LAURIE'S CHILDHOOD AND YOUTH: ALBANY AND NORTHAM.

My father, Laurence Leonard Dowling, was the 5th child and fourth son, and was born in Albany on the 9th of September 1915. There were five children in the family under the age of seven years. Ellen his mother, was just 24 years of age and fortunately she loved babies and showered them all with love and affection, as much as could be expected of a mother with five young children. She was remarkable in her care and support of them, particularly because her husband was often away for long periods driving trains in different parts of Western Australia.

Laurence Leonard Dowling: *A man for all seasons.*

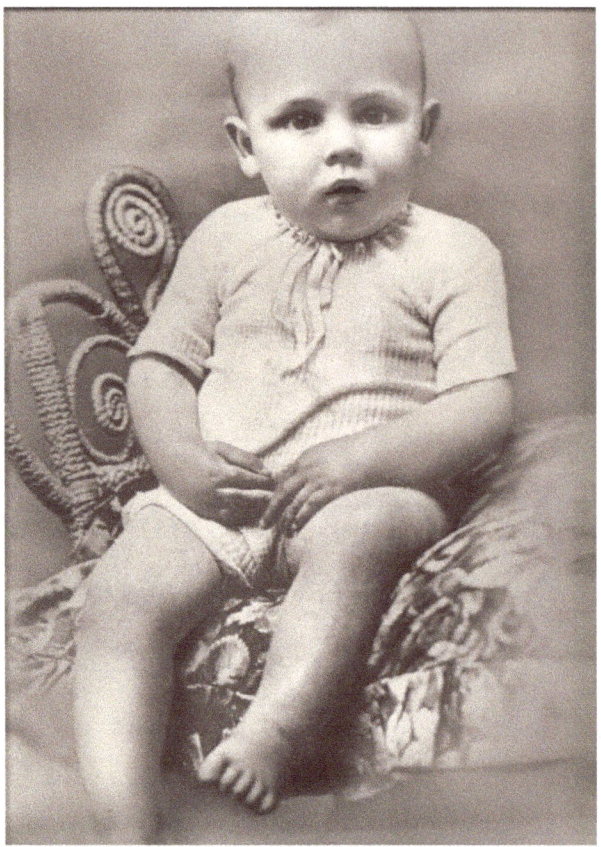

Image 11: Laurence Leonard Dowling: aged 1.

Laurie always adored his mother and the bond with her was very close. He looked a great deal like her with his blue grey eyes, and dark brown hair while his father was blue eyed with fair hair. Some siblings have suggested that he was her favourite child. He was born with an independent spirit and grew up with a three older brothers and one sister. The older brothers taught him to swim early by simply throwing him off the jetty in Albany, but he was fortunate to swim "like a fish" they said. They roamed the bush and supplemented the meagre family budget with bush honey and fish that they caught from the sea, wild rabbits and any other bush foods that they could find. By 1927, when Laurie was 11 years of age, he had 8 surviving siblings. The family was still growing and another was expected. He and his siblings attended the Albany convent school.

Image 12: Laurie and his older sister Eileen and younger brother Mack at the Albany convent school

Much to the family's dismay in 1927, they were moved to Northam by the railways' department. This town is approximately 99 km from Perth to the east, on the road to Kalgoorlie. The harsh wheat belt climate was in contrast to the cool coastal town of Albany. Northam was noted for its extremes in temperature. Burning in summer, freezing in winter. In those days Northam was the heart of the railways in Western Australia and could be described largely as a railway workers' town peopled by the poor Catholic Irish who worked primarily in the railways, the police force or labouring jobs. The flour mill was in the heart of town, grinding away 24 hours a day, a reminder to the poor of their insufficient sustenance.

Image 13: Northam looking from the Avon River and towards the flour mill
https://www.aussietowns.com.au/town/northam-wa

There was a large indigenous population in Northam also poverty stricken, hungry and outcast by society. Here Laurie's family joined the community of train drivers who received a living wage to feed a family of 4 children but inadequate if you had 8 children. There was never enough food to go around and there was no coastline for fishing. Often they went to bed hungry and his mother on reminiscing said: "I didn't know where the next meal was coming from". Laurie's closest sibling Eileen remained the only girl in a family of 8 boys and he loved her greatly. Being a couple of years older than himself, she cared for him as best she could. As they grew older their joint task was washing and wiping mountains of dishes, a job Laurie detested as he wanted to be outside roaming the bush with his older brothers and admitted that he often tried to annoy Eileen, so she would send him outside or his mother would intervene and send him away. Laurie recalled that although his mother was extremely nurturing and kind she did not tolerate any nonsense. If the boys had fights among each other, his mother who was built to last the long distance would "wallop" them into shape. She was always fair he said, but she did not tolerate misbehaviour from her brood of boys. Each of the children in this growing tribe of children were expected to look out and take care of the younger ones beneath them, even if only a couple of years younger. The family bonds were strong, loving and supportive and in face of their grinding poverty everything was shared as fairly as possible.

By age 11 though, Laurie was shouldering responsibility to shoot wild rabbits for the family meals. He shot the first feral fox to enter Western Australia and received a bounty of ten shillings. The family feasted for days upon the welcome windfall, and his mother was very proud of his achievement. She did her best to make life good for her brood; she sang and played music on an old piano each evening. There was abundant love and warmth growing up despite a deficit of food, clothing and education. Much of their clothing was made from old flour bags, and shoes and boots were a luxury. At the age of ten, Laurie received his first pair of boots and was so proud of them that he wore them to bed every night. The children were born at home and the family had little access to medical or dental services so you learned to live quietly with pain. Even in his worst moments of pain as an adult, Laurie never made a sound. He had grown up that way.

All the boys attended the local convent school. The sisters of St Josephs of the Apparition opened St Josephs School in 1889 in Northam. Laurie liked learning, but found school somewhat humiliating as weekly the nuns would line up all the children whose parents had not paid the school fees. He was always on the line as well as his brothers and sister. Without enough money for food, school fees were never going to be paid. To be fair, the nuns were probably poverty stricken as well, as St Joseph's was part of a poor Irish Catholic community.

As soon as Laurie turned 12 years of age, it was time to leave home. The school teachers pleaded with his mother not to terminate Laurie's schooling. He was highly intelligent, performed brilliantly in all subjects, and played the violin by ear and the piano: gifts he inherited

Laurence Leonard Dowling: *A man for all seasons.*

from his very musical mother. He could write poetry and prose with a fluency that astonished his teachers and his mother said she was related to the great Scottish poet, Robbie Burns and was certain that was the source of his literary talents. In all, the Dowling family was to produce 11 children who grew into adulthood. All with different talents but literature and writing was talent shared by several of the siblings and later their children.

Image 14: Laurie Dowling's family with his parents and the 11 siblings who survived to adulthood. From right to left by seniority.

Laurie soon discovered that childhood was short lived among the poor. Being an independent provider for oneself was valued and it bred a tough independent type. His oldest brother had left home to learn to drive trains at the age of 12 years; his next brother, Wally, became the most famous drover of cattle on the Canning stock route. He was moving herds of cattle through the Great Sandy Desert from Wiluna to Halls creek a 1000 mile trek through some of the harshest desert in the country.

Image 15: the Canning stock route
Ref: https://www.pinterest.com.au/pin/canning-stock-route-put-this-on-your-bucket-listrememberthis-is-not-for-the-cry-babies

Wally had a reputation in the cattle industry for toughness and kindness. He often rode bare foot and had once walked 500 miles

Laurence Leonard Dowling: *A man for all seasons.*

across a blazing desert to save his horse. He had wept when he saw the Aborigines perishing of starvation during the long droughts of the 1950's and the incursion of cattle into their country who ate their scanty food. Once he found a dying aboriginal baby on the breast of his dead mother, and he couldn't leave it there to die. He nursed it on camel's milk and called him Pelican. He knew his mother would have been pleased. Pelican became his head stockman, with the finest skills of any stockman he had ever met. Again he found another 3 year old aboriginal on the desert track, left to starve by his dead parents and he also raised him calling him Church-hill. He made friends with the aboriginal people and employed them on his teams whenever he could. He often spoke about how during the great famines of the 1950's, if he killed a bullock for the teamsters and they left the bones and hide behind that within a few hours the aboriginals would have taken everything, even the blood on the ground, so desperate were they for survival. He had a big heart like his mother, was tough like his mining ancestors with independence, resilience and bush nuance that were extraordinary. He once mended his own broken leg with greenhide. Like his Irish ancestors he had a way with horses and they always remained his closest companions. He died of influenza at Mistake Creek when he was just 49 years of age. He claimed that he also fought during World War 2 in the Middle East, Greece and Crete and was wounded, but survived. Some family members dispute this saying his role of bringing cattle to the meatworks was an essential service during the war and he was exempted from military service. Amid his toughness, he was a poet and below is one of his poems used as the lyrics for one of Slim Dusty's songs.

Dr Patricia Sherwood

Blackened Quart Pots Are Boiling
by *Slim Dusty*

Down the Wave Hill Track they're coming
Twelve and fifteen hundred strong
And the lonely nights are gladdened
By the watcher's lifting song
Dusty pads are wearing deeper
Wearing deeper as they wind
For the Vestry's mobs are walking
With the Bull's heads close behind
Baldies, shorthorns, wild eyed pokers
Mobs of ev'ry breed and brand
From the wilds of Westyern Australia
To the Barkley Tableland
While the bullocks from the Gulf runs
Are walking with the rest
And the battered, blackened quarts are boiling
On the stockroutes North and West

Down the river now they're stringing
To the flats of channel grass
And the Brumbies wheel and whistle
As the bullocks slowly pass
Swinging down the lonely stages
As the dust wrack swings aloft
From the rolling downs of avon
To the hills of Yelvercroft
Mobs for sale and mobs for fatten
On the river flats inside
Oh, the good old days still linger
When the outback drovers ride

Laurence Leonard Dowling: *A man for all seasons.*

Slowly mobs are feeding campwards
As the evening shadows fall
And the battered, blackened quarts are boiling
In the twilight overall

By the plains and scrubs and rivers
Where the western stars burn bright
The friendly fires are glowing
In the drover's camps tonight
While the bullocks from the gulf runs
Are walking with the rest
And the battered, blackened quarts are boiling
On the stockroutes North and West
On the stockroutes North and West

From his album: "The Best of Slim Dusty"
Songwriters: Wally Dowling, Joy McKean
Contributed: Marten Busstra 2009

These poems captured the glory and harshness of the outback with a droll humour and contentment that both amuses and challenges the imagination.

Slim Dusty wrote an Eulogy to Wally Dowling's tenacity and endurance, to his pioneering spirit and his indomitable spirit in the ruthless outback. Wally represented a pioneering spirit that broke and made men and women who tried to conquer the inhospitable lands of Australia.

Dr Patricia Sherwood

End Of The Canning Stock Route
by *Slim Dusty*

The camp gear's in the storeroom, all the packs are in the shed
With the dust of seven summers on their hide
Saddle straps are hard and brittle, stirrup irons are rusty red
For the Canning Stock Route finished when Wally Dowling died;
No more cattle travel southward through the spinifex and sand.
All the wells are falling in along the track
Now the Cannings but a legend, just a lonely desert land
And it's doubtful if the Munjongs want it back.

Eight hundred miles of sandhills, now and then a sandstone ridge
With a salt lake here and there with samphire flat;
An oasis in the desert you can find at Durba Spring,
Bubbling, running water, it's a fact;
But unless you own a camel, you could never travel there,
And a horse would fail now the wells have fallen in.
For the sandhills on the Canning reach a hundred feet or more
And it's certain that no car could take you in.

The famous 'Never Never' and the place they call 'Outback'
Two elusive lands that few men ever found
Are located on the Canning down that lonely desert track
Where to be this very moment would be worth a thousand pound.
To be with Wally Dowling, whipping water from the well,
While the stockmen hold the mob back from the trough,
Stop the thirsty bullocks trampling in their great desire to drink.
Just to do one trip would suit me well enough.

But my wish is just a daydream, which can never be fulfilled,
For when Wally died the stock route had it's day.

Laurence Leonard Dowling: *A man for all seasons.*

Now the Billaluna cattle are travelling down to Broome
In a roaring diesel roadtrain, to the meatworks by the bay,
And the tick line stops the others, every station in the north.
No one may use the Canning if he would;
So they truck their beef to Wyndham and sell for what it's worth;
And I doubt they'd use the Canning if they could.

It's really had its day now and won't be used again,
No more drovers horse bells ringin' will be heard,
For the cattle loaded road train, smothered in its diesel fumes,
Now struggles up the rise in lower third.
When I travel up the Canning, I am sure to be alone
With my camels and some thoughts of yesterday.
They will take me slowly northward, 'til at last the trip is done,
And find contentment when I've stowed the packs away.

The camp gear's in the storeroom, all the packs are in the shed,
With the dust of seven summers on their hide
Saddle straps are hard and brittle, stirrup irons are rusty red
For the Canning Stock Route finished when Wally Dowling died;
From his album: "Things I See Around Me"
Songwriters/composers: Peter Muir; Slim Dusty;
Contributed: Marten Busstra 2009

Image 16: Wally Dowling with his mother.

Wally was Laurie's look alike. Laurie idolised him and they both shared characters of independence, extraordinary survival talent and a combination of kind heartedness, generosity and toughness that is rare. Their religion was life, their altar the outback and their peace was found in the great silence of the deserts surrounded by the raw materials of nature and survival. Towns and cities had the temptations of grog used to shield their sensitive souls from the loneliness that echoes through empty urban streets. They were both happiest in the outback, embraced by the ambience of solitude and silence.

Laurence Leonard Dowling: *A man for all seasons.*

Like Wally, Laurie left school at 12 years of age and was given a swag, food for a meal, a pair of boots and waved goodbye. It was up to him to find a way in the world and to survive. His family had gifted him life, love and warmth but economic poverty made it a necessity to leave so the younger ones could be fed and clothed. Laurie had learned the ropes from his four older brothers (his sister remained at home until she turned 15 years and then was expected to get married quickly. In the meantime she was the house help for the following 8 siblings.) He jumped onto the back of a slow moving train and hung to the outside of the last carriage. His brother had made Meekatharra way up north and joined a droving team. He hoped to reach it too. This was the way to travel when you had no money. Eventually you would be spotted by the train's guard and thrown off. But, Laurie only made it to Wubin, in the heart of sheep/wheat country north of Northam and near Dalwallinu about 272 kilometre from Perth, where he walked to a farm offering to work in exchange for food and keep. He lived off rabbits and boiled wheat, camped under the stars or in the shearing shed. He learned all the skills of wheat/sheep farming but loved working with the horses best. When he was 14 years of age, he received his first pay and used it to have all his teeth removed as due to poverty and no dental care he had suffered greatly from toothache in his childhood and early youth. He then headed north and undertook droving for a while and helped out on any cattle stations that needed a stockman. He was an asset to any station as he applied himself to repair as well as maintenance. He could fix cars, repair plumbing, and undertake electrical work. There was nothing he was not willing to turn his hand to or his intelligence to master. Once he even rebuilt a car on one f the stations in which he worked.

But he was also young, unsettled and searching for something. He returned to Northam where he was offered an apprenticeship as a butcher. He hated the work but it was a steady job and income. And the great depression had hit his generation hard. Many were unemployed and battling to survive. He considered himself fortunate. When he was 19 years he married Eileen Ethel Browning and a son was born in 1935 who was called Terrence Leonard Dowling and whom they both doted upon. He was a sunny child and brought great joy to them both. They lived in Northam where they were both close to their families. It was a tragedy that later Terrence, who was extremely hard working, died shortly after accidentally falling from a roof he was repairing, when he was only 43 years of age. He left a wife and three beautiful young children.

In the meantime, into their marriage came the Second World War, that disrupted the lives of millions, caused the death of millions and damaged the bodies, hearts and minds of so many. In 1939, Laurie was enlisted in the $2^{nd}/7^{th}$ regiment of gunners in the 9th division. He was just 24 years of age and says it was the first decent paying job most of the young men of the depression generation were offered including himself. He had not reckoned on the costs to his personal health, his emotional life and his marriage. Although he was tough physically, mentally very strategic , quick thinking and acting, these traits would not protect his sensitive soul and heart in the bloody heartless battlefields.

CHAPTER 3

THE WAR AND ITS FALLOUT

There are no winners in war before or after, for the mental, emotional, and physical damage leave deep scars upon the survivors, their families and future generations. Laurie Dowling belonged to a generation where politicians tried to glorify war and young men were convinced that it was the honourable way to defend their country. So Laurie Dowling and many other working class lads from Northam voluntarily joined up and were assigned the 2/7th field regiment which was initially assigned to the 9th division, to defend the British interests in the Middle East. The regiment's fields of action are described below:

> In November 1940 the regiment was concentrated at Fremantle and deployed to the Middle East aboard the troopship *Stratheden*. Arriving there in December,

Laurence Leonard Dowling: *A man for all seasons.*

the regiment moved to Qastina in Palestine, where it undertook training, albeit without any equipment or vehicles, which were in short supply in the theatre as the British sought to make up losses in home regiments following the Fall of France.

As such, it was not until April 1941 that the regiment received a supply of vehicles and its first artillery pieces. These came in the form of a mix of antiquated 18-pounders and 4.5-inch howitzers. These were replaced in July with twenty-four 25-pounders when the regiment moved to Mersa Matruh,[7] which it employed against German and Italian forces in defence of the garrison at Tobruk and then later around Halfaya Pass–Sidi Barrani before being withdrawn back to Cairo, in Egypt, where they undertook a training role from October 1941 to early 1942. During this time the regiment trained reinforcements for British and Commonwealth artillery units in the theatre and undertook daily shoots on the Almaza firing range.

A move to Syria followed in February and for a while the regiment was based around Tripoli and then Aleppo where they were assigned to support the 20th Brigade as they undertook garrison duties following the successful Allied campaign against the Vichy French government. The regiment remained there until the middle part of 1942 when the regiment was committed to both the First and Second Battles of El Alamein. (Ref: https://en.wikipedia.org/wiki/2/7th_Field_Regiment_(Australia)

Dr Patricia Sherwood

My father frequently referred to himself as one of the "Rats of Tobruk" and in more lighthearted moments as Lawrence of Arabia. He liked the Middle East, liked the locals and said he felt at home there. He was familiar with the desert country from his time in the outback of Australia and thought middle eastern food was delicious. At other times, he laughingly said that the only difference between himself and an Arab was that he washed a little more frequently and he had photos of himself dressed as an Arab. My father praised the German soldiers as fine fighters and said he admired greatly their strategies and skills and especially the tactics of their General Rommel. There is some dispute over the fact that Rommel in turn is reported to have said:

> If I had to take hell, I would use the Australians to take it and the New Zealanders to hold it.

However, the dark side of the Middle East haunted my father forever after. His best friend and mate died next to him. He was mortally wounded and Dad would recall trying to push his mate's intestines back into his stomach while trying to save his own life and that of his other mates in his regiment. He tried to commemorate his mate's death in poetry:

> To My Mate
> We buried Frank in Ataman
> In the desert land so far away
> With the rest of the boys of the fighting ninth
> Who died with you that tragic day?
> We left you Frank in a foreign land neath a small white cross and the rising sun

Laurence Leonard Dowling: *A man for all seasons.*

The proudest badge in the world today
The badge of the man who beat the Hun
We told your Mum and Dad old man
How you fought and died in the hell of a day
They are mighty proud of their soldier son
But Neath brave smiles their hearts are sore
Tis a year today old fried
That you died that we might live
Greater love hath no man...

He was haunted by the tragedy of it all as the death toll rose and the horrifying deaths of his companions occurred before his eyes. During his funeral, many years later, several of his army mates came up to me to say that they owed their lives to his quick thinking decisive action. In 1943 he was mentioned in dispatches in London for his bravery and courage in defending his mates and his regiment and was awarded an oak leaf.

By the KING'S Order the name of
Gunner L.L. Dowling,
Royal Australian Artillery,
was published in the London Gazette on
24 June, 1943.
as mentioned in a Despatch for distinguished service.
I am charged to record
His Majesty's high appreciation.

Secretary of State for War

Dr Patricia Sherwood

As my father was quick thinking and decisive in his actions, he never waited for orders, and he rapidly sized up the situation and acted for life and survival. The glory and glow of the war propaganda began to crack through his patriotic soul when after the defeat of Rommel, he with some of his regiment, were sent to collect the Germans' guns and ammunition. He was shocked to find that the Germans' guns were made by the same manufacturer as his divisions' guns. It was then Laurie said that he realized there were bigger players in the war than governments or soldiers. There were clearly international business interests busy making profit out of the conflict and suffering.

Laurie used to recount with calm the journey back to Australia in 1943 saying they were lucky to avoid German warships and/or submarines in the Indian Ocean and to arrive back safely in Fremantle. They were then hoarded into cattle trucks and began the long dusty journey across the Nullabor plain to the Atherton tablelands where they were to be trained for jungle warfare. Even today with sealed roads it is a 12 day driving journey. One can only imagine enduring weeks on the dusty deserted, unsealed roads across Australia. Laurie really loved the Atherton tablelands saying that is was one of the best parts of Australia that he had ever had the privilege to see or to camp in.

The jungle warfare and particularly the Kokoda trail Laurie recalled with horror. He was wounded in the stomach but survived, contracted malaria and amoebic dysentery like so many of his mates. He says they fought half dead from tropical diseases and poor food. He expressed contempt for the Americans saying they had terrible survival skills and did not look before they shot into the jungle. He was more concerned about being killed by American soldiers in the jungle than by the Japanese soldiers. The 2/7th was then assigned to in 1945 to clear out the remainder of the Japanese in the pacific islands nearby:

Laurence Leonard Dowling: *A man for all seasons.*

Assigned to the 26th Brigade which was to capture Tarakan, in April 1945 the regiment was moved to Morotai Island. The day before the main landing at Lingkas on 1 May, the 57th Battery landed on Sadau Island, where they established themselves to fire on Lingkas to provide cover for engineers that were tasked with clearing the beach obstacles. ...Guns from the 2/7th Field Regiment fire along with Matilda tanks from the 2/9th Armoured Regiment at «HMAS *Margy"*.

The following morning the battery fired in direct support of the seaborne assault; it was the first time ever that a unit of the Royal Australian Artillery was ever employed in such a role. Once the beachhead was established amidst some confusion caused by muddy conditions and congestion, both the 13th and 14th Batteries came ashore and by 4:00 pm on the first day, they were both in action, while the 57th was also moved to Tarakan from Sadau late in the day. Small parties from the 2/7th also took over control of naval gunfire support after the naval shore fire control parties were withdrawn at the end of the first month. Over the next three months they would fire over 37,000 rounds in support of the 26th Brigade's three infantry battalions this included rounds from a captured Japanese 75 mm mountain gun.

(https://en.wikipedia.org/wiki/2/7th_Field_Regiment_(Australia)#:~:text=The%202%2F7th%20Field%20Regiment,of%20El%20Alamein%20in%201942.)

Laurie did not gloat in victory over the Japanese. He recalls that the Japanese soldiers were fleeing back to Japan, a ragged and under resourced group of men, malnourished and in fear and terror. He deeply questioned the bombing of Nagasaki and Hiroshima where so many innocent men, women and children died. From his point of view it was both callous, cruel and unnecessary for the Japanese were clearly defeated and on the run home. He described it as the cruellest experiment upon civilian populations he had ever heard of and completely unnecessary.

Laurie, like all war survivors who have witnessed so many horrors, atrocities and deaths of mates and friends, did not return to Australia the same young man who had left. His physical health was ruined and he carried to his death remnants of gunshot in his stomach. Mentally, he like the many others, had undiagnosed PTSD which they managed with excessive alcohol consumption. Others were completely broken and were said to be "shell shocked" wandering about with incoherent babbling. It was naively assumed that the men who had encountered such darkness in the human soul, been subject daily to life threatening violence and destruction should return to pick up the threads of their pre-war lives as if nothing had happened. On his arrival home, he went to see his mother and sister who say he came back "a different person" damaged by the horrors of war at a level that they could not believe possible. He tried to visit Frank's parents and tell them the story of their son's last moments. He took the train to Kojonup where they lived but when he alighted at the station, he could not face telling them the horrors and anguish of their son's death. He waited for the return train. He could not reveal to them the truth of Frank's slow agonizing death. It was enough that he had witnessed it. They must never know the horror of it.

For Laurie, like so many returned soldiers, post war attempts to fit back into their pre-war family were disastrous. After 6 years apart from his wife and son, he came home to a family he did not know

Laurence Leonard Dowling: *A man for all seasons.*

and who did not know the man he had become, hardened and given to alcohol to assuage the grief and loss of it all. It was not surprising that the marriage collapsed and he found himself alone seeking itinerant work on stations and farms and in between times engaging in destructive benders. He tried his hand at many things, mining asbestos at Wittenoom Gorge, working in the abattoirs in Wyndham, fishing in Shark Bay but his restlessness kept driving him on. There was little peace til he took up prospecting for gold again in the Kalgoorlie hinterlands. He found solace in the quiet of the bush, away from the noise and bustle of the cities. He was now 30 years of age and of no fixed address. Eventually he was to re-find his feet and stability and in 1952 took over the ownership of the butcher's shop in Kondinin , a remote wheat belt town on the edge of the Western Australian desert heading east towards the rabbit proof fence and just before Hyden and its famous Wave Rock. His decision to locate there was to shape the future of his life and become the beginning of my life.

Image 17: Kondinin: heading toward Hyden and the rabbit proof fence

CHAPTER 4

A SECOND START: MARRIAGE AND A NEW FAMILY.

Kondinin was to prove a turning point in my father's life. He was 40 years old and while operating his butcher shop in Kondinin boarded at the local hotel as was often the custom in those days. There he met Lucy Torrisi. She was stunningly beautiful, dressed like a Hollywood film star as the locals commented.

Laurence Leonard Dowling: *A man for all seasons.*

Image 18: Laurie and Lucy: wedding day.

She was unmarried at 34 years of age. She had migrated from Sicily at the age of 7 years with her family to escape Mussolini in 1929 and she became the first Italian woman migrant in Western Australia to become a school teacher. She had previously rejected many offers of marriage and instead had chosen to pursue the love of her life which was a teaching career. In those days a woman had to resign the moment she married. Also she had been her father's major confidant and carer in his older years and regularly devoted her holidays to travelling back to Newlands, near Donnybrook to see how he was faring. He had died in 1953. She was a very popular teacher at the Kondinin School and had been reminded by the inspector that year that if she wished to have a family, it was about time she started looking. Lucy had attended many country dances, balls and social events but had never become engaged to or involved with any man. She recounts that when she first met Laurie at the hotel where they boarded, she was attracted to the flowers he always had in the window of his shop as she was a great lover of fresh flowers and gardens. As it happened the two became a pair and were engaged. Lucy, my mother, was transferred to Mt Many Peaks School to set up the school but they both remained steadfast in their commitment and married in May of 1954 in Belmont at the local Catholic Church where Laurie's mother now lived. Mum purchased all the furniture for her family home and my father bought a family home at 53 Rankin Street Kondinin, a stone's throw from the local hospital and just across the road from the local Catholic Church. I was born 10 months later and was much wanted by my mother and deeply adored by my father. Fortunately during her pregnancy, she refused to take thalidomide for her morning sickness that was prescribed to her, so I was born whole and healthy, arms and legs as they should be. Dad wanted to call me Ellen after his mother, but my mother vetoed that and called me Patricia as all the Patricia's she had taught were lovely girls and Mary after her mother. At that time, my father's son Terry from his first marriage was also staying with our family as he had been taken on as a butcher's apprentice by my father. During this time, a teacher shortage occurred in Kondinin and the Education department begged Mum to go back to teaching even allowing me to go to school with her which I am sure I would have thought great fun. However, my father in his traditional male role prohibited my mother from returning to work, arguing that he would look diminished in his community as if he was unable to support his family. My mother capitulated as was the norm in those days. She became very active in the Catholic women's community and my father with the men who maintained the church. They both had high hopes for their union except that my mother complained that occasionally my father drank a little too much when he spent time with his mates at the local hotel. Mum was teetotaller and into healthy food and diet. She ensured that Dad ate plenty of vegetables with his meals to address the deficiencies in his diet.

Laurence Leonard Dowling: *A man for all seasons.*

When I was 10 months old she became pregnant with my brother. This marked a turning point in their marriage. Firstly my mother nearly died giving birth to him as she bled profusely post partum. The nurse told her the last woman had died from blood loss and that this was the doctor's first appointment, so he was not very experienced. She demanded they call Laurie who came immediately and was horrified. He exclaimed to the doctor and nurses: "Never have I seen so much blood even when I kill a bullock. If you don't stop the bleeding immediately I am calling the flying doctor service now to take her to Royal Perth Hospital". The doctor was admonished into action by my distraught father and they gave Mum multiple injections until the bleeding stopped but she was so weak afterwards, she needed home help for 3 months post my brother's birth. Throughout her life she said that she owed her life to Laurie's quick action and commands that he gave at the Hospital. However, she felt that Laurie never really bonded with the child whom he wanted named Frank after his fallen mate. As a concession she named him Francis Brian, but always called him Brian.

Then disaster happened. My mother's experience was that when Brian was only 10 months old and I was just over two years, the bailiff came knocking at the door to reclaim the furniture and informed her that the house was to be sold because the Butcher's shop had gone bankrupt. She was devastated. Laurie's view was that his son from his first marriage, Frank, who was completing his butchering apprenticeship with him, had been stealing from the till and passing the money to his mother. He never forgave him unfortunately, and they never reconciled. Terry's untimely death from a tragic accident at 43 years of age was received by my father without any obvious emotional response. That was common in my father; he suppressed emotions, internalised grief and loss and had continuous ulcers and gut issues throughout his life. When situations became too difficult emotionally he went bush and sought solace in the silence of nature or simply withdrew into a silent unreachable world. The collapse of the business was a tragedy for everyone. Dad's health had a complete breakdown as he internalised stress and his ulcers were so bad he had to be hospitalised in Perth. Mum was left alone to manage with a 10 month old and a 2 and half year old. Fortunately she had a small inheritance from her father so organised a removalist truck to take our furniture to Perth and rented a dreary tenement in Bulwer Street near Hyde Park, long before it became a fashionable residential location. I remember the long journey in the removalist truck and I really disliked the grey sandy soil in the back yard of my new home as I was used to red earth. I was repelled by this grey house that had bats inside and the round rambunctious landlady who used to visit weekly to collect the rent scared me. The neighbourhood was full of disadvantaged families and the children next door stole my toys. Mum begged for a teaching position as a relief casual which was granted and then on that basis and her inheritance, made an offer on a lovely house in Eton Street, North Perth. She no longer spoke about my father. It was as if he had simply vanished. Later I found repeated letters written by my father to my mother trying to find a way forward after his discharge from hospital to which she never replied. She made the decision that she had to go it alone and when he was discharged he went north seeking work in the seasonal fishing industry before he returned to our new home a year of so latter. When Dad returned we had a thriving vegetable garden, 15 fruit trees of all sorts which Mum had planted in our backyard, chickens and a rabbit run. While Mum worked, we were cared for by pensioners who in exchange for food and keep minded us during the weekdays.

Finances were never Laurie's strong point. He had grown up with a survival consciousness living day by day, helping those poorer than you and it never changed. It was the source of much chagrin with my thrifty mother. When Dad returned he worked again in the butchering business finally establishing his own business. Mum complained

Laurence Leonard Dowling: *A man for all seasons.*

regularly that he would give meat away to the poor children without charging. She said this extreme generosity also contributed in her view to the initial bankruptcy in Kondinin as well. She despaired that Dad would give someone "the shirt off his back" if he met someone in need. That was my father though; his heart was always open to those who suffered because he knew what it was like to be poor and hungry, an experience unknown to my mother. She regularly told my brother and l, that "if it was left to your father, we would be living in tents on the street." Although she only earned half a man's wage as a relief teacher she was industrious, frugal and very careful with money and expenses. She tutored children at night to make ends meet. In this way they were extreme opposites. I remember my Dad, trying to help when l came running into their bedroom at night because l was scared of the dark, and Mum would become very cross. He even made me a tiny 5 watt lamp to turn on at night but l was devastated when Mum made him remove it as it "wasted power". I always defended my Dad's kindness and generosity in face of my mother's criticisms but l also felt deeply for her distress every time the bailiff came to our house with a court order to repossess our furniture or house. Mum had to keep receipts for every single item in the house and show them repeatedly to the bailiffs who caused her much stress, humiliation and anguish. There was an unbridgeable chasm between them when it came to household expenses and money matters.

They were united though by a shared a love of flowers and our flower garden was magnificent with roses, gladioli, ranunculus, carnations, zinnias, poinsettias, frangipanis, camellias and they sent flowers to the church for the Altar regularly. They also both had a really classy clothing style and whenever Dad had money he bought the best tailor made suits. My mother also dressed exquisitely and when Dad had money he bought her the most beautiful jewellery gifts which were testimony to his love of beauty and his deep love for her.

Dr Patricia Sherwood

Then the alcohol hit again and Dad started staying out at the hotel later and later. Eventually I witnessed a loud accusatory fight between them when I was 5 years old. My mother was pointing to lipstick on a white shirt and my father was saying something about never having sex anymore. Then it ended with the wedding photo being smashed by my father, collecting his clothes in a small bag and kissing me goodbye. Thereafter I only saw him on some weekends, and my mother obtained a formal separation in the courts. Sometimes he organised outings for us and sometimes we went to the house of another woman who was kind to us. I remember the joy of Dad taking me to the Perth royal show and buying me a doll. I also remember the heartbreak of waiting for hours on the front fence for my Dad who just did not arrive at all, or who arrived so drunk that he could barely relate to me.

In 1963, after another failed butchering business, Dad went to work on the railway gang putting down the rail link across the Nullarbor Plain, one of the most desolate parts of Australia. The railway gangs only came home for Christmas. I was devastated and could hardly function with the loss of contact with my father. I had been dux of years 1 and 2 at school but failed every subject in year 3. I simply couldn't think. I cried myself to sleep and depended on Dad sending me glorious mementos from nature in the desert, everlasting flowers, a huge maroon and gold beetle, a special rock, or an unusal seed pod. I kept them in a treasure box, which was an old gold biscuit tin, but which I took out regularly whenever I was missing my Dad and looked at my treasures. Then my cousin and brother decided to bury my treasure box one day in our quarter acre back yard and refused to tell me where. I was hysterical and received no justice or sympathy from my mother who described is as "just an old tin". I decided to seek justice from my Dad although he was so far away. We wrote weekly but were only able to tell him good news. So I planned it all well. I found an old envelope and wrote dad's address on it c/o post

Laurence Leonard Dowling: *A man for all seasons.*

office Widgiemooltha, a remote town south of Kalgoorlie. I told my Dad how much I missed him and I needed him to come home again, of the treasure box tragedy and how my heart was so sad without him. I collected empty bottles from the street and traded them for a stamp and secretly posted my letter. I trusted my father to be the arbiter of justice and a few weeks later a letter arrived for me from my father with a ten pound note and a threat to give my brother a cousin a hiding when he came back to Perth if they did not return my treasure box. My mother was horrified that I had so much money and had worried my father. The trouble is she would say: "You are just like your father, too emotional too sensitive, too excitable to cope with this world." This letter was a turning point in the marriage and my little 8 year old life.

At the end of that year, Dad returned and made major efforts to rekindle the marriage. Mum agreed as long as he attended AA and I had the happiest two years of my family life. Mum bought a car. We had Sunday picnics, went on bush walks picking wildflowers, laughed as a family, cooked toasties over hot fires at night, and Dad would tell me all about the stars in the sky at night and the different constellations like Orion's belt, the Southern Cross, the Pleiades, Sirius and Venus. He could read directions from the night skies something that he learned as stockman in the pastoral stations out back. Sometimes we read Banjo Patterson's poetry or Henry Lawson's poetry. From my father I developed a great passion for Australian literature, especially the bush poets that Dad so dearly loved. His capacity for literature and writing was remarkable. He particularly loved Mark Twain's novels as well as the writing of Joseph Furphy and the short stories of Banjo Patterson. He wrote very beautiful letters, poetry and prose and could memorise any book he had read a couple of times as he had a photographic memory. Later when we attended rehabilitation services which held family quiz nights for patients and their families, Dad won every quiz as anything he read or heard he remembered. I recall him reading me *Such is life*, *Pickwick papers* and *Uncle Tom's cabin* by rote without needing the book. Mum always praised this incredible gift of writing and the photographic memory held by my father. It was a gift I shared up to the end of primary school. Then it gradually declined.

It was a tragedy for Dad, so creative, so gifted and so intelligent that he lacked the education and qualifications to get jobs suited to his abilities. Mum understood this and always felt it was the cause of much of his dissatisfaction with life. When I was 9 years old Dad worked in a heavy machinery place in Welshpool and always came home black and exhausted. Eventually he had enough of that and in my 10th year he obtained lighter work as a mail sorter in the GPO. He found the work profoundly boring but his health was deteriorating quickly as he reached 50 years and the war injuries were now becoming chronic. He had surgery to remove part of his ulcerated intestine and we made frequent family trips many Sundays to the veteran's hospital in Perth, Hollywood where Dad spent recurrent visits and much time.

He gave up on AA and the alcohol problem returned with a vengeance. He was so disabled that he was granted a TPI (Totally and Permanently incapacitated war pension). Unfortunately, that meant that he had money to purchase alcohol for 7-9 days a fortnight and was only sober for the rest. During his alcoholic binges he drank port wine, vomited regularly and talked incessantly about the horrors of war, rambling about his mates dying in the trenches in Tobruk and pushing his mate's intestines back into his stomach while trying to save his own life. Enough to make any passerby within earshot a pacifist. Dad lived in the sleep out permanently now. Mum cooked and cleaned for us all, paid all the bills and suffered his alcoholism and occasional verbal abuse. He was never violent and it was always my job to sit him down and try to get him to eat or help him get into bed. Mum worried constantly about his lack of food intake and his ill-health. He smashed the car that Mum had purchased, had a drink driving conviction which mortified Mum and she sold the car. Family

Laurence Leonard Dowling: *A man for all seasons.*

life was hopelessly flawed again with a cycle of alcoholic binging until Dad was hospitalised for a few months, only to be released to begin it all over again. When he tried to make a break, he would go bush to the peace of the goldfields, searching for gold and prospecting like his ancestors. Dad often said that he was searching for Lasseter's lost reef of gold, somewhere out there in the great deserts of Australia where he felt so at home.

On the good days, I had some wonderful conversations with my father that shaped my life. We spoke about the big issues of life: death and dying and the purpose of life. He always had humility around these questions and often said we don't know all the answers to these, we are still all searching, trying to make sense of the suffering around us. I remember crying in his arms when my long term pet cat Monty died when I was 14 years old and asking him why those we love have to die. While Dad was not highly religious, he did love the rosary and it was one of his few possessions when he died.

Laurie was also a strong Labour party man and I learned my early class analysis and politics from Dad. He also spoke to me about trade unions and the working man's life and the need for politics to right the wrongs of economic and social injustice. We talked about great labour leaders and I once won a prize for an essay I had written about Bob Hawke, inspired by conversations with my father when Bob Hawke was a leader of the ACTU. I had predicted in 1971, that he would become a future prime minister and he did so in the 1980s. Dad's deep commitment to kindness and generosity, and to his view that no-one should go hungry or homeless inspired my social justice vision and the many projects I devoted myself to as an adult to address these inequities that my father had spoken of to me.

Laurie's other great love was for his mates who had survived in the 2/7th regiment and with whom he had spent so much of his most traumatic years fighting for survival. Every Anzac day they met and shared memories of mates who did not survive, of experiences in which they did survive. At my father's funeral so many men came and told me that they owed their lives to my father's quick thinking actions and leadership. Dad never waited for orders. He saw a problem and he addressed it immediately. He manifested that truly great Australian outback spirit where no-one is coming to rescue you. You need to be innovative and decisive in your actions to survive in situations that will often have life and death consequences. He was truly a courageous man and a great team leader because he always had his eye on the weakest, the one which most needed to be protected and supported. How different his life would have been if he had not been denied an education through poverty, nor had his soul scarred by the battles of an unmerciful and vicious war.

When I was in my final year of High School, my brother persuaded my mother to have the legal separation renewed and Dad was homeless again. My brother had never bonded closely with my father and in turn my father found it difficult to understand my brother's reluctance to help around the home or find part time work. I was devastated when Dad left but as I had a car and could drive on weekends I would visit him wherever he was living. Firstly I visited him in Pinjarra helping out an old war mate on a dairy farm and where Dad was living in a hut. We had great conversations, often went for drives together and he shared driving tips with me. Later however, he ended up living in pubs which in exchange for his pension provided alcohol and lodging until his pension was exhausted. I was now trying to locate my Dad at different city pubs and being a sensitive 17 year old, hated the way the men in the bars leered at me when I enquired as to my father's whereabouts.

The next year I went to the Eastern states, to the National University in Canberra feeling I needed a break from my family role as the rescuer and carer. I jumped into the first relationship that came my way and married a 37 year old divorcee who turned out to be

Laurence Leonard Dowling: *A man for all seasons.*

violent member of the Russian Mafia, holed up in hiding in a remote town in NSW where I was literally imprisoned for the next two years of my life. Without access to a phone, I heard the tragic news in a letter from my mother that my father had had a massive stroke, diagnosed with Korsokoff's syndrome caused as a result of chronic alcohol consumption and Vitamin B1 deficiency. Dad had entirely lost his short term memory and recognised nobody but Mum. He was in Sir Charlie Gardiner Hospital and doctors thought he would not survive. Eventually another letter arrived saying he had survived but had permanent short term memory damage and that he was to be admitted to Lemnos hospital for permanently mentally disabled and traumatised soldiers. It was both a refuge and a hell hole for my father. A refuge because he had a bed, regular meals and medical attention and there was no alcohol.

Here though the hidden acute and chronic PTSD from the horrifying Second World War prevailed as hollow Men wandered around shrieking intermittently, "shell-shocked" I was told... or mumbling incoherently to themselves, hallucinating or ruminating respectively over horrifying unprocessed war experiences. Others wandered in a soulless silence, haunted by ghosts that they alone could see. Nobody but nobody was capable of a coherent conversation but my father. Laurie could have intelligent conversations, and his long term memory was excellent. He also recovered his recognition of family members. He had intense insight into his suffering and mental problems. It was truly the hellish depot for Second World War veterans/survivors in an era that had failed to recognise the massive psychological damage inflicted upon the men who had fought in the battlefields, and witnessed unspeakable atrocities. Rarely were there any visitors, so rarely that a visitor's name was recorded by the staff so when the inmates died and family members came claiming their assets, they would be able to provide evidence as to whom had actually cared for the inmate.

My father survived because of my mother's loyalty. She had him home every Sunday for the day, cooked his favourite foods and kept him up to date with family happenings. She fought the soulless bureaucracy and administrators at the hospital for rights for my father: for good reading glasses, dental care, good clothes and better food. She never gave up on his welfare. She also insisted he be provided with a library of books to read during the long days of the week when he had no one with whom to converse.

My father was like a caged bird and hated it. He was freedom loving soul who had roamed the outback and loathed being so confined. Once he escaped and was found several days later on the way home to my mothers. He had sought refuge with the Salvation Army when he had become lost. He always admired the "Salvos". He often said that they were the real helpers on the battle fields, in the pubs and where the homeless and poor lived. He would know. He had experienced those places first hand. Occasionally his sister would visit him, and of course his loyal 2/7th army mates came too. Brian visited when as my father said "he wanted money from him". Dad who had always been penniless was finally a man with some savings as a result of his war pension being accrued for him weekly.

When I returned to Western Australia, I visited Dad regularly at Lemnos, and we walked in the nearby park grounds, fed the birds and shared old memories. At first I wept with him over my tragic first marriage in which the ex mafia husband had disappeared with my first born. Dad re-assured me: "She has Dowling genes, she will be tough and she will survive and you will be re-united one day." And later, Dad proved to be right. By that time some OT options had opened up at Lemnos, and Dad made a variety of wooden tables, beautifully crafted, and tried his hand at other crafts. Everything he did was like the work of a skilled craftsperson.

Laurence Leonard Dowling: *A man for all seasons.*

Image 19: Dad at 64 years showing me his latest craft creation: a beautiful macramé pot plant holder.

Dad was immensely proud of my educational achievements for I was blessed with all the opportunities he had been denied. In 1984 when I graduated from the University of Western Australia at 29 years of age with my PHD, Dad was there to congratulate me despite his failing health at 69 years of age.

Image 20: Dad congratulating me at Eton Street following my PhD graduation.

Dad had developed a serious smoking addiction from fourteen years of age, aggravated by his wartime experiences and his level of stress. He continued to smoke endlessly, 40 cigarettes a day had been his smoking diet for decades. This was clearly another attempt to calm the inner anguish and stress. Not surprisingly he developed emphysema which was to be his Angel of death.

When I married and moved south to a hobby farm near Boyanup, I would have Dad come and stay with me for a week at a time, so he could experience again being close to the bush and nature. Dad though had become very emotionally fragile and told me if he had to kill his own meat he would become a vegetarian, well before it was fashionable. He just could not attend his mother's funeral or visit her in her aged care home saying that he was "not up to it". His spirit was so scarred by life's battles that that his skin was almost translucent and his soul life quite fragile. He was now quite breathless and every step

Laurence Leonard Dowling: *A man for all seasons.*

cost him his life-force. His body had carried enough suffering, seen enough pain, borne enough grief and loss, carried so many burdens that it was time to return to his maker.

It came very unexpectedly one spring. The hospital rang to say he was ill and would I like to come and see him, as I usually did although it was a three hour drive. I made it a priority. I asked them how serious did they think his illness and they replied: "oh he could live another 2 months, 2 years, nobody can tell." Twenty minutes later they rang to say he was dead. He had died of undiagnosed pneumonia. His had not cried out in his suffering, he had not complained. He had simply quietly died without anyone to show any concern or kindness. That was my father. No matter how much pain he was in, he never ever called out for help. His level of endurance was beyond understanding. Only when he collapsed did anyone know he had a serious problem. I was shocked and insisted they leave his body undisturbed until I arrived to say my final good byes. When I arrived I went straight to his room. I always remember holding his hand and looking at my hand. Both were the same shape... those long, long fingers and slender wrists and when I looked upwards, I saw his beloved mother, already in the heavens holding his other hand and welcoming him home to a place of rest, peace and healing. I knew it was my turn to carry on the gifts that he had given me upon this earth: his perceptive intelligence, his keen sensitivity, his writing giftedness, his pursuit of justice, his generosity of spirit and his courageous soul even against all the odds and his stalwart capacity to survive.

His funeral was held five days after his death on the 2nd October 1990, and his body was buried at the Catholic Lawn cemetery in Karrakatta, where his mother and father's bodies were also buried. My mother was there standing in silent grief over the death of the only man she had ever loved and seeing the culmination of their broken dreams but unbreakable bond. Her incredible devotion and faithfulness until the end of his life was extraordinary. He always remained her husband, the only man she had every given her heart too. She always reminisced about the good times they had and grieved for the lack of opportunity he had encountered in his life to fulfil his incredible potential.

He had a soldier's farewell with the last post played by the remnants of his 2/7th regiment, and the surviving rats of Tobruk turned up to farewell one of their number. They expressed gratitude openly to the man who had saved so many of their lives. Later Bill Woods sent a personal letter to my mother of condolences in which he wrote: "Laurie is remembered by his signaller comrades as a soldier full of resourcefulness and determination to get things done when the pressure was on-his mention in Despatches is testimony of that". The service concluded with a rendition of the "Lord is my Shepherd' and in honour of his cultural and spiritual heritage his headstone consisted of an ornate Celtic cross with the simple inscriptions: "A generous and loving man, a courageous and valiant soldier".

Image 21: Laurence Leonard Dowling's headstone.

Laurence Leonard Dowling: *A man for all seasons.*

My grief was so great, that days passed afterwards without me knowing where I was, which day it was or the time of day, til one day my crying was interrupted when I heard a voice singing to me in my kitchen:

> *Hush, little baby, don't you cry; Papa's going to sing you a lullaby. Hush little baby don't say a word; Papa's going to buy you a mockingbird.*
> *If that mockingbird won't sing, Papa's going to buy you a golden ring. If that gold ring turns to brass, Papa's going to buy you a looking glass.*
> *If that glass begins to crack, Papa's going to buy you a jumping jack. If that jumping jack is broke, Papa's going to buy you a velvet cloak.*
> *If that velvet cloth is coarse, Papa's going to buy you a rocking horse. If that rocking horse won't rock, Papa's going to buy you a cuckoo clock.*
> *If that cuckoo clock won't tick, Papa's going to buy you a walking stick. If that walking stick falls down, you'll still be the sweetest little baby in town!*
> **Ref:** http://americanenglish.state.gov/reso...

I knew it was my father's voice, because he had sung this song to me when I was a small child to comfort me if I showed any distress. I looked upwards and there he was in the spiritual world, radiant and peaceful at last and I asked him why he went without saying goodbye to me. He said that he could not have left his body if I had been there. I would have kept him here and his body was worn out and he needed to let it go. He said he would be around for the next 12 months and he would help me in all the ways that were within his power. After 2 years he said he would have to go a long way away and could no longer communicate with me.

In the 12 months following the death of his body, I felt his spirit working on my behalf. After 10 one year contracts, I was given suddenly out of the blue without application permanency at University. And my motherhood dream which had been shattered by the disappearance of my first child, Elizabeth by her violent mafia father was restored when at last I met her again. My heart was healed though by a new gift of motherhood at 37 years of age. Little did I know, but at the time of my father's death I had just become pregnant with my son David John. His father, John and I decided when he was born on the 5th June 1991 to call him David John Laurence Sherwood to honour Laurie's gifts to his ancestry. Like my father, he has grown to be tall, thin, wiry, highly intelligent , deeply perceptive and a sensitive soul who definitely inherited much of my father's Celtic heritage of strength, willingness to explore new horizons, quick thinking and the courage to take on leadership in challenging moments and to continue the work for justice and equity. David John Laurence has been blessed with a life of opportunities educational and economic that were unavailable to my father. He was awarded the prestigious Rhodes scholarship and attended Oxford University where he became recipient of one of their coveted business start-ups and has remained in England, the land from which his great, great, great Irish grandfather migrated to Australia. David John Laurence remains a reminder to our family of some of the brightest qualities of Laurence Leonard Dowling, my father, his maternal grandfather and truly "a man for all seasons".